W9-APF-792

REFERENCE

Library Media Center
Addison Central School
Addison, N.Y., 14802

DRUGS ON
YOUR STREETS

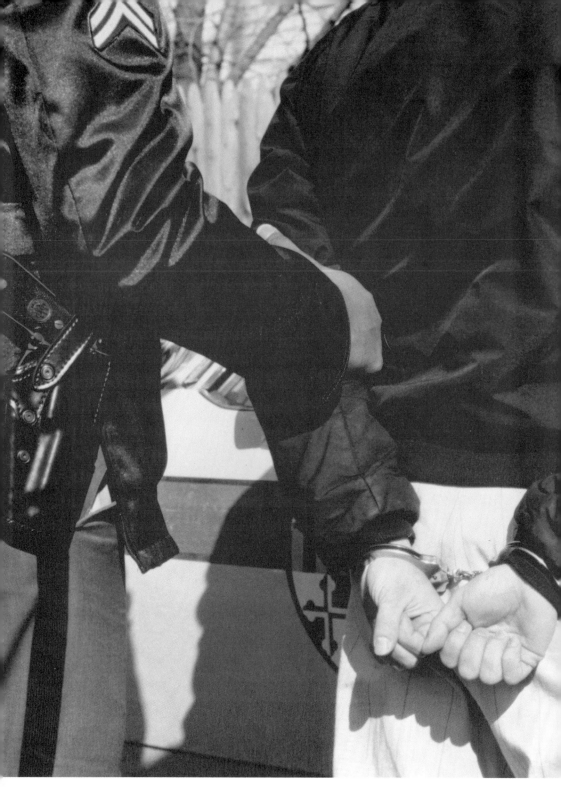

Trying drugs can lead to a downhill slide from using to dealing to arrest and jail.

THE DRUG ABUSE PREVENTION LIBRARY

DRUGS ON YOUR STREETS

Gabrielle Edwards

THE ROSEN PUBLISHING GROUP, INC.
NEW YORK

The people pictured in this book are only models; they, in no way, practice or endorse the activities illustrated. Captions serve only to explain the subjects of photographs and do not in any way imply a connection between the real-life models and the staged situations.

Published in 1991 by The Rosen Publishing Group, Inc.
29 East 21st Street, New York, NY 10010

Copyright © 1991 by The Rosen Publishing Group, Inc.

All rights reserved. No part of this book may be reproduced in any form without permission in writing from the publisher, except by a reviewer.

First Edition

Printed in Canada

Library of Congress Cataloging-in-Publication Data

Edwards, Gabrielle I.
    Drugs on your streets/Gabrielle Edwards. —1st ed.
    (The Drug Abuse Prevention Library)
    Includes bibliographical references and index.
        Summary: Discusses various drugs and their dangers and presents survival techniques for existing in a drug-infested neighborhood.
    ISBN 0-8239-1267-1
        1. Drug abuse—Juvenile literature. 2. Drug abuse—United States—Juvenile literature. 3. Drugs—Physiological effect—Juvenile literature. [1. Drugs.
    2. Drug abuse.] I. Title. II. Series.
    HV5809.5.E38 1991
    362.29—dc20   91-18369
                                 CIP
                                 AC

Contents

Introduction

*B*ecoming involved with drugs is foolish. Others get rich on your misery. Misery is the only return that drug abuse pays on your money. Some drug abusers die from drugs. Some go insane. Others are robbed of their human qualities.

On the streets we see the effects of drug abuse. Young people look like the walking dead. Their cheeks are sunken. Their bodies have shrunk to skin-covered skeletons. They eat from garbage cans and sleep in the streets. Nobody wants them. Drugs have taken their lives.

Drugs are all around you whether you live in a big city, a small town, or a village. Someone there will sell you misery and suffering for life.

The purpose of this book is to tell you what is out there in the streets. Street drugs are illegal because they are so harmful. Alcohol and tobacco are legal drugs. They are harmful to body and mind also. Think about yourself while you read this book. Think of keeping your life whole.

Cocaine has become a major killer on American highways.

Drugs affect all the workings of the body—even the ability to
make an easy pool shot.

CHAPTER 1

What Are Street Drugs?

*F*ood nourishes your body. The food you eat helps body tissues to grow and repair themselves. Food gives you the energy you need to keep your body organs working.

Drugs are not food. Drugs do not supply your body with nourishment or energy. Some drugs are medicines used to cure diseases. Medicines are legal drugs. To buy some of them, you need a doctor's prescription.

Drugs sold on the street are not medicines. These drugs are called *psychoactive* drugs because they change a person's behavior.

10 The brain controls behavior. Some behavior is inborn. You accidentally prick your finger on a pin and pull your finger away. No one taught you to do so. It is reflex behavior. Other things that we do are learned. You get up each day at a certain time. That is learned behavior.

Abused drugs affect the brain. When taken into the body, they reach the brain. Some drugs affect the brain for only a few minutes. Others stay there longer. But all psychoactive drugs change behavior. In street slang, the user becomes *high* or *stoned*. People who take drugs lose control of their minds.

Abused Drugs

Drugs sold on the street are illegal. They are very harmful.

Some of the abused drugs come from plants. We call them *natural* drugs. Street drugs that come from plants are heroin, crack, cocaine, LSD, and marijuana.

Synthetic drugs are made from chemicals. Among the synthetic illegal drugs are angel dust (PCP), uppers (amphetamines), and downers (barbiturates). All of these drugs affect the user's behavior. They mess up the brain. They turn the user's

emotions upside down. They make the *11*
unreal seem true.

Most of the illegal drugs affect the user
in physical ways, too. Some users develop
peculiar ways of walking. Many perspire
even when cold. Drugs affect the heart
rate. Some drugs slow the heart. Others
speed it up. Drug users become ill quite
easily.

Drugs interfere with your ability to
think and to make good decisions. Drugs
damage your mind and your body.

Getting wasted is the worst way to cope with your problems.

Many drug addicts first get into the habit of using by going to the family medicine cabinet.

CHAPTER 2

The Danger of Trying Drugs

You cannot trust drugs sold on the street. You know that street drugs are made illegally.

Over-the-counter medicines and prescription drugs usually affect the same person in the same way. There is no guessing about the reaction. For example, most people can take aspirin to relieve a headache. However, aspirin upsets some people. That is because people's body chemistry differs. The drug is the same. The working of the body differs. Medicines made by formula are safe when used as directed.

13

14   They are not made with concern for quality. Drug dealers cannot tell you where their drugs come from. They do not know who made the drugs or how strong they are. They do not know what chemicals were used to cut (dilute) the drugs.

In fact, drug dealers do not care if you live or die. The stuff they sell may be pure or laced with poison. There is no way to tell until it is too late.

Dealers Make Addicts

Street drugs are very powerful. Taken into the body, they work on the brain and its nerves. The brain and its nerves are called the *central nervous system*. Use of a street drug becomes a habit with a user. People who cannot control their need for drugs are called *addicts*. A person who must use drugs is said to be *addicted*.

Drug dealers want to get you addicted. The street term for addicted is *hooked*. A hooked person is a drug dealer's source of income—until the addict is jailed or dies.

Drug dealers use dishonest ways to get people hooked. A drug dealer will give you drugs free until you cannot do without them. Once you are addicted, you are willing to pay any price. You are enslaved by the dealer and the drug.

Addicts Become Pushers

Anyone addicted to drugs must get money for a fix as often as needed. Most addicts steal from family, friends, strangers; from anyone and anywhere. Many addicts become drug pushers. They sell drugs in the street. They push drugs on younger children to get money for their own supply.

Caught up in the drug business, addicts become dishonest and dangerous. They often sell fake drugs. Addicts may fill capsules with talcum powder or baking soda or poison. Sometimes they fill capsules with poison. Like the dealers who sell to them, addicts do not care if a buyer lives or dies. They sell drugs, real or fake, to get money to supply their habit.

Don't Try

There is no such thing as experimentation. You cannot take the chance of experimenting with your life. One use of a drug may addict you. Drugs will overpower you. They will condemn you to a life of suffering.

Drug users may become paranoid—afraid of their own shadow.

CHAPTER 3

Angel Dust

*A*ngel dust is a sly name for a terrible drug. Its real name is ***phencyclidine,*** or PCP for short. On the street, angel dust is also known as crazy dust, dust magic, goon, rocket fuel, and cyclone.

Legally PCP is used as an animal anesthetic. You may have seen on television how scientists inject a wild animal using a dart gun. The PCP quiets the animal. When the PCP wears off, the animal suffers no harmful effects. That is not so with humans. People who use PCP suffer horrible effects.

No one can guess how PCP will work in the body besides making a person high.

18 Angel dust may affect the same person in different ways at different times.

When angel dust is taken into the body, it is stored in the brain. In some people it remains in the brain for months. PCP stored in the brain can cause *flashbacks*. A flashback brings about the full effect of the drug even though a person has not used it in a long time. Repeated flashbacks can make a person go insane.

Use of PCP

PCP is produced as a pill or capsule, in powder form, and as a liquid. The powder form may be drawn in through the nostrils. That is known as *snorting*. The powder is also sprinkled on marijuana and smoked. In liquid form PCP is injected into the bloodstream.

Angel Dust Violence

PCP often causes a kind of insanity that leads to suicide or violence. PCP brings on *hallucinations*. A teenager believed that flies were attacking him. To escape the imaginary horror, he jumped off a roof and was killed instantly.

Some angel dust users become violent. The drug gives them a false sense of strength. While high on PCP, a user may try to fight off imaginary attackers.

CHAPTER 4

Marijuana

*O*n the street marijuana is known by a number of names. The most common street name is *pot*. The nickname comes from the Mexican name of the hemp plant, *potagua ya*. The scientific name of the plant is *Cannabis sativa*.

Marijuana Is a Dangerous Drug

The dried leaves of the hemp plant are ground up. They are then rolled in a paper wrapper like a crude cigarette. A marijuana roll is called a reefer or joint.

At one time marijuana was not thought to be as harmful as other drugs. We now know that it is very dangerous.

19

20   Marijuana contains 61 psychoactive substances called *cannabinoids*. The most important of these is delta-9-THC.

When a person smokes pot, the delta-9-THC travels from the lungs into the blood and the blood carries it to the brain. It dissolves in the fatty tissues of the brain and those of the ovaries and testes.

Effects of THC

Scientific evidence shows that daily pot smoking affects human behavior. THC damages the cells and changes the way they work.

Marijuana smoking makes people unable to remember things from one minute to the next. That is called short-term memory. School grades fall when a student's short-term memory fails. Eventually, a daily user of marijuana is not able to concentrate. A person cannot learn if concentration and short-term memory are lost.

When a person smokes marijuana, THC is carried throughout the body by the bloodstream. Some of the THC is left in the ovaries and testes. It is believed that THC causes brain damage in the babies of parents who use marijuana.

Marijuana users lose interest in achieving anything in life.

Marijuana, the Enemy of Youth

Marijuana is not your friend. Dr. Walter Lehmann is a medical doctor who specializes in treating teenagers. He made a study of 3,000 teenage boys and girls who had become hooked on drugs. Dr. Lehmann says that the effects of marjuana use are at first hidden.

When a person smokes pot, THC remains in the body from five to eight days. Pot causes gradual changes in the working of body cells.

22   Marijuana controls the smoker. Gradually a decline in personal habits takes place. Learning ability begins to fail. School grades begin to fall. Energy decreases. The smoker's appearance becomes sloppy.

Heavy pot smokers develop a mental illness. Concerned only about smoking pot, they lose all desire to do anything else. Feeling the need to get a better high, many pot smokers move on to hard drugs.

The smoke of marijuana is full of chemicals that injure the entire breathing system. The tissues that line the air passages in the nose and the bronchial tubes leading to the lungs become infected. That results in bronchitis. Regular pot smokers suffer chronic sore throat. Even worse is the hardening of the lungs that causes *emphysema*.

Hashish

Known on the streets as *hash*, hashish is a stronger variety of marijuana. The cannabis plants grown in Africa and the Middle East produce stronger chemicals. Like marijuana, hashish is smoked. Hashish causes all the trouble that marijuana does in faster and harsher ways.

CHAPTER 5

LSD

The initials LSD stand for *lysergic acid diethylamide*. LSD is made in chemical laboratories. The drug is a hallucinogen. At first it was used by psychiatrists to treat *schizophrenia,* a mental disorder in which the unreal seems real. Unethical persons moved LSD into the street drug market.

LSD looks like water. But it does not react like water. A drop of liquid too small to be seen through a magnifying glass can cause violent hallucinations.

In the street LSD is known as acid, beast, cubes, ghost, and micro dots. LSD is dropped on a sugar cube or a micro dot of paper.

24   As a person takes in LSD, changes occur in the body immediately. The pupils of the eyes open up. The heart begins to beat very rapidly. The blood pressure increases, and the muscles tighten. Within one half hour after taking the drug, hallucinations begin. The series of hallucinations is known as a *trip*.

LSD makes the user "see" brilliant yellows, reds, oranges, and purples. Objects

Ordinary things can look strange and terrifying to a person on an LSD trip.

seem to glow with an overpowering brilliance.

Persons hallucinating on LSD receive confused brain messages. They "hear" colors, "see" sounds, and "feel" thoughts from tables and chairs and paintings. The LSD trip often turns terrible and frightening. The user may feel that his or her head is separated from the body. Cockroaches may seem as big as elephants. The images may be so terrifying that the person panics. LSD can drive a normal person insane. The damage caused by the drug may be lasting.

Other Hallucinogens

Like LSD, other drugs cause hallucinations. *Mescaline* comes from the peyote cactus plant. In street slang it is known as peyote, cactus, buttons, beans, and big chief. Another drug, *psilocybin*, comes from a variety of mushroom. On the street it is called mushrooms, Mexican, and magic.

Both of these drugs can make users dependent upon them. In strong doses they have been known to cause panic. Persons in panic may hurt themselves or others.

Cocaine users make elaborate preparations to snort a line of coke.

CHAPTER 6

Cocaine

*C*ocaine has a long and evil history. In the 1880s the use of cocaine was widespread. It was considered to be a tonic. Makers of soft drinks put cocaine into soda pop to give their customers a pleasant lift. The drug was put into medicines made to treat asthma, hay fever, corns, and the common cold. By 1900 the bad effects of cocaine began to be seen. By 1903 laws were passed in the United States declaring cocaine an illegal drug.

What Is Cocaine?

Cocaine is a drug found in the leaves of the coca plant. This plant grows in the countries of Peru, Bolivia, and Colombia.

28   In the street cocaine is called coke, c, snow, blow, nose candy, toot, happy dust, flake, base rock, and bernies. No matter the name, cocaine is a dangerous drug. It addicts people. It causes hallucinations.

Cocaine is a white powder. Pure cocaine is very powerful. A dose the size of a green pea will kill. Because it is so powerful, pure cocaine is cut before it is sold. Other substances such as baking soda and a sugar called dextrose are added to it. Some people cut cocaine with talcum powder or even poison.

How Cocaine Is Used

Cocaine may be taken into the body in three ways. It may be snorted, or inhaled. Many users snort a thin line of the powder through a straw. When snorted, the drug passes through the moist membranes of the nose into the small blood vessels. The effect of the drug is felt in a few minutes.

In liquid form, cocaine is injected into a vein. That is called *mainlining.* When treated with petroleum ether, cocaine can be smoked. In this form it is called *freebase.* When cocaine is injected or smoked, its effects are felt immediately.

Cocaine is a stimulant. That means that it makes the user feel "up" or excited.

People say that it makes them feel happy, that it gives them energy, that it helps them solve problems. Those feelings are false. For about half an hour the user may feel happy, self-confident, powerful, and vigorous. Then depression sets in. A depressed person may feel confused, angry, anxious, and sad.

To rid themselves of depression, users take more cocaine. The cycle of false happiness, depression, and use continues. In that way, users become psychologically (mentally) dependent on the drug. Psychological dependence leads to addiction.

Pushers hang around schoolyards hoping to snare new customers at an early age.

30 | *Dangers of Cocaine*

Cocaine actually attacks the body. It can cause dangerous changes in blood pressure, chest pains, and heart attacks.

Very young cocaine addicts may suffer strokes. The person may lose the ability to speak, to walk, or to control body functions. Cocaine may cause seizures or hallucinations.

Pregnant women who use cocaine give birth to addicted babies. These babies are underweight and ill. Many are brain-damaged.

Cocaine has become a killer on the highway. A recent study showed that one in four traffic deaths is caused by a driver who uses cocaine. Cocaine changes the way people hear and see things. It changes their ability to act in emergencies. The unreal becomes real to cocaine users. The drug makes them believe that bugs are crawling under their skin. Cocaine makes some people *paranoid*. A paranoid person imagines that others are plotting against him. He can become violent because he always feels threatened.

Everyday noises sound overly loud to cocaine addicts. Cocaine can turn normal happenings into frightening experiences. Should cocaine menace your life?

Junkies spend most of their time shooting up—or thinking about it.

Supporting a crack habit is an expensive proposition.

CHAPTER 7

What Will Crack Do to Me?

*O*n the East Coast it is called crack. On the West Coast its name is rock. On either coast dealers may push it as bat or cookies or turbo. The name doesn't matter. Crack is just a quicker way to get hooked.

Crack is produced in *crack houses*. Cocaine is heated in a way that changes it into a solid, crystal-like substance. This crystal sheet is broken into chips or rocks.

Crack is a very powerful drug. It is almost pure cocaine. It may be white, yellow-white, tan, or brown. Usually crack is packaged in plastic vials about an inch in length. It is also sold in foil wrap and in envelopes with a see-through window. Many young people become hooked on crack using it the first time.

34   Crack is smoked. Chips can be smoked in a marijuana joint, in a tobacco cigarette, or in a pipe. The cocaine vapors go directly to the lungs, then into the bloodstream and to the brain. In about five minutes the smoker feels intense pleasure. The high lasts from five to seven minutes. It is followed by a downer or crash so terrible that the user will do anything to get more crack.

Crack dealers lure first-time users by telling them how cheap the drug is. Crack is not cheap. People who are hooked on it crave the drug intensely. Many users smoke crack several times an hour. Addicts may go on binges that last three or more days. Imagine supporting a habit that costs $25 an hour!

Crack attacks the brain very quickly. The blood pressure rises. The heartbeat increases dangerously. Some users have heart attacks. The breathing rate increases. In some cases, the respiratory system fails. Some people have convulsions. Others die during muscle seizures.

Like cocaine users, crack addicts have a change of personality. They become paranoid, believing that others are "out to get them." They have hallucinations. Crack addicts can become violent.

Crack and Babies

An expectant mother can damage her baby by smoking crack just once.

When a pregnant woman smokes crack, the vapors travel through the blood stream and are deposited both in her brain and her womb. As the baby develops in the womb, it is exposed to crack.

Crack settles in the brain, preventing normal development. Brain-damaged crack babies are learning-disabled for the rest of their lives.

Some crack-exposed babies are born with damaged hearts and with sight and hearing defects. Many have difficulty learning to walk. Babies born with crack in their systems will need care for the rest of their lives.

Moonrock

Moonrock is crack mixed with heroin. It is smoked. Crack smokers use moonrock to prevent the crash. The result is that they become addicted to both crack and heroin.

Drugs in a neighborhood make everyone feel nervous and threatened.

CHAPTER 8

How Crack Destroys Neighborhoods

When crack has taken over a neighborhood the signs of invasion are everywhere. Empty crack vials lie on the sidewalks and in the gutters.

Crack changes the rhythm of a neighborhood. There is too much activity day and night. Very young people drive around in flashy cars belonging to drug dealers. Cars with out-of-state license plates cruise the neighborhood, too, looking for a drug dealer.

A crack neighborhood is full of people who just "hang out." They idle on street corners, in parks, and on stoops. They stand in front of "grocery stores" that really sell only drugs.

38 Another kind of "store" is the crack house. Abandoned buildings are taken over by dealers. There they turn cocaine into crack. Crack may be sold in the crack house, and addicts smoke it there.

Organized groups that sell crack are known as "gangs," "crews," or "posses."

In the gang or posse people have special work categories. The *lookout* watches for police. A *hawker* advertises drugs for sale. Children may be used for both of those jobs. A *steerer* is responsible for locating buyers and spotting the undercover police officer. Teenagers fifteen years and above are used in this work. *Runners* as young as ten are used to carry messages between gang members. The *stasher* hides the drugs for the seller. The *seller* handles the actual sales.

When crack takes over a neighborhood, violence follows. Fights explode between gangs. They are really neighborhood wars. Gang members are killed. So are innocent people. People who live in neighborhoods where crack has taken over live each day in fear.

CHAPTER 9

What Are Narcotic Drugs?

*N*arcotic drugs cause drowsiness in the user. They relieve pain. But there is a terrible side to some painkillers: They addict those who use them.

Opium

The opium poppy is the source of a family of natural drugs. All of these drugs are painkillers. All are addicting.

The opium poppy grows in the hot, dry climates of Turkey, China, India, Iran, and Mexico. Sap from its seed pods is collected. This sap is raw opium.

Legal Opiates

Drugs made from opium are called opiates. At one time several legal painkillers were made from opium. Morphine is

39

40 one of those drugs. During the Civil War morphine was widely used to ease the pain of wounded soldiers. So many men became addicted to it that laws were enacted to limit its use.

In very small amounts morphine and other legal opiates are still used in prescription medicines. One is *paregoric*, which is used to treat diarrhea. Another is *codeine*, which is used in cough medicines. However, codeine has become part of the illegal drug trade. On the street it is known as school boy. When abused, codeine is addicting.

Heroin, the Illegal Opiate

Heroin is made from morphine. On the streets heroin is known as horse, junk, hard stuff, smack, H, and dope. Heroin is indeed dope. It is addicting and mind-destroying. It may even kill.

Heroin may be taken into the body in four ways. In powder form, it is snorted into the nasal passages. Most heroin addicts inject dissolved heroin into a vein, which is called mainlining. Some addicts inject the dissolved drug under the skin, which is called skin-popping. Recently, addicts have been mixing heroin with cocaine and smoking it.

Like other illegal drugs, heroin affects the brain. It slows the activity of the part that controls involuntary body functions. Involuntary functions include breathing and heartbeat.

Mainlining junkies have needle tracks along their inner arms and outer legs where heroin was injected.

Junkies share needles. These dirty needles carry the germs of infectious diseases. Diseases commonly found among heroin addicts are blood poisoning, hepatitis, syphilis, malaria, and AIDS. AIDS is now the leading cause of death among heroin addicts. A woman addict with AIDS passes the disease to the baby in her womb.

Methadone

Methadone is a synthetic drug. It is used to decrease the need for heroin. Methadone is still being used to treat heroin addiction. There is a down side to the treatment: Methadone is itself addicting. The person under treatment has to be withdrawn from methadone.

A teenager on stimulants pushes himself beyond his physical limits.

How Are Stimulants Abused?

*S*timulants are drugs that *stimulate* the central nervous system. They make brain cells work faster. They also speed up the activities of body cells. Any drug that affects the brain changes moods. Any substance that changes the mood is dangerous.

Amphetamines

The *amphetamines* are a family of stimulants. Their street names are uppers, speed, bennies, arrows, and pep pills. Members of the family are dextroamphetamine (dexies) and methamphetamine (crystal meth). The amphetamines are synthetic drugs.

43

44   The use of amphetamines became quite popular. Doctors prescribed them for appetite control and to treat alcoholism. They were used in the treatment of overactive children. Benzedrine inhalers were used to clear clogged noses.

Amphetamines work on a certain group of brain cells. When stimulated, these cells give off a chemical that makes body cells work faster. Amphetamines make people feel full of pep and more alert. When the drug wears off, depression takes over. The user then takes pills again and again to keep the peppy feelings.

People misuse amphetamines to hide feelings of hunger or thirst or to stay awake. Amphetamines may be obtained with a doctor's prescription. They are sold on the streets illegally.

People who abuse amphetamines become hyperactive. They are restless and easily excitable. They become angry and want to fight. They have hallucinations. Many abusers show signs of paranoia, becoming afraid of others. The muscles tremble. The pupils of the eyes close, even in the dark. The eyes are unusually bright.

Amphetamines are taken into the body in two ways. In pill form they are swallowed. In liquid form they are injected.

Abusers of amphetamines become psychologically dependent. They have a strong mental urge for the drug. Amphetamines are also physically addicting. The body tissues require daily amounts of the drug.

Amphetamines drive people to do things beyond their physical limits. Believing that he could walk on water, an amphetamine abuser drowned. Many addicts become murderous. The depression caused by these drugs is unbearable. Many people become suicidal. Heavy doses can cause a complete breakdown.

Withdrawal from amphetamines is long and difficult. It must be done under a doctor's care.

Ice, the New Family Member

Methamphetamine is an "old" member of the amphetamine family. Illegal chemists have changed its structure. The new form is known as *ice*. Ice is smoked.

An ice smoker remains high for a day. The crash is terrible. The symptoms of the crash are like a mental breakdown. Victims hallucinate. Some are unable to speak understandably. Some become violent and have to be restrained.

46   Ice causes body and brain cells to over-work. Users are unable to sleep or eat. They lose a great deal of weight. The body temperature rises to dangerous levels. The heartbeat loses its normal rhythm. Ice kills.

Ecstasy

Ecstasy is a mixture of amphetamine and synthetic mescaline. It is taken by mouth. Ecstasy causes hallucinations. It is a mood changer. It may produce nausea. Some people become suicidal after using the drug for a long time. Some users have flashbacks.

Crank

Crank is crystal methedrine, an amphetamine. It is also known as speed, fast, quick, and ups.

Crank stimulates the central nervous system. Users are called *crank heads* and *speed freaks*. Crank is snorted, injected, or mixed with beverages. People who inject crank go on binges. They go without sleep for a week or more. Users may suffer from paranoia. Crank kills.

CHAPTER 11

What Are Depressants?

Mood-changing drugs become abused drugs. Drugs that change moods act on the central nervous system. Stimulants excite the brain and its nerves. Body activities are quickened. *Depressants* slow down body reactions.

Barbiturates

The family of the *barbiturates* numbers about 2,500. Barbiturates are made legally in standard formulas. Each formula is designed to treat a certain ailment.

The barbiturates are used as sedatives. Sedatives relax the central nervous system. Before surgery, they are used to make the patient sleepy. Some barbiturates help to control conditions such as high blood pressure, epilepsy, and ulcers.

47

48   Barbiturates are sold also in the illegal drug trade. On the street they are known as downers, goof balls, barbs, candy, blues, and many other names.

Barbiturates are swallowed in capsule or pill form or dissolved in liquid and injected into the veins.

Some barbiturates act on the body for a short time. Others act for a longer time. The effect of the short-acting barbiturates is like that of alcohol. Users become "drunk." They stagger and become unbalanced. Their speech is slurred. They are confused about time and place. Some people become very irritable. They withdraw from others.

Withdrawal from barbiturates must be under the supervision of a medical doctor. An addict may die if withdrawn too quickly.

Tranquilizers

Valium, Quaalude, Librium, and Miltown are tranquilizers. They are used to calm people down. However, they are very addicting. The signs of abuse are like those of the barbiturates. The treatment for tranquilizer addiction is long, hard, and costly.

How Does Alcohol Affect Health?

*A*lcohol is as old as the human race. Early humans made alcohol from grain. Beverage alcohol is still made from grain. Whiskey is made from corn and rye. Wines are made from fruit juices. Beer is made from grain. Alcoholic beverages are rated by strength. A strength rating is called *proof*. Strong alcohol has a high proof number.

Alcohol goes from the mouth to the stomach and the intestines, which absorb it. Alcohol goes into the bloodstream and to every important body organ.

Alcohol knocks out the brain center that receives messages. False messages are received that change behavior. Alcohol

50 causes mental confusion. The person staggers. The speech is slurred. Some people become violent. Others fall asleep.

Organs that help remove alcohol from the body are the liver, kidneys, lungs, and sweat glands.

The liver is the largest gland in the body. It is necessary for life. One of its important functions is to remove harmful substances from the blood.

Too much alcohol in the blood over-loads the liver. When that happens, other chemical activities are delayed. Energy is low. That brings about a drop in the blood sugar level. Fat builds up in the liver.

Alcohol destroys liver cells, and scar tissue takes their place. Blood cannot flow through scar tissue. A reduced flow of blood through the liver causes the serious disease called *hepatitis*.

Cirrhosis is another liver disease caused by heavy drinking. Cirrhosis of the liver leads to death.

The digestive tract processes the food that you eat. Alcohol harms the digestive tract. Cancer of the mouth and throat are linked to alcohol and tobacco smoking. Alcohol inflames the food tube and the stomach lining. Heavy drinking leads to stomach ulcers.

Heavy drinking ruins the heart. The heart pumps blood through the body with great force. Constant drinking of alcohol lessens that force. Irregular heartbeat occurs and causes shortness of breath. Sometimes the heart becomes enlarged.

Heavy drinking causes disease in the blood vessel that leads from the heart. The person feels pain in the chest, which is a symptom of heart attack.

Alcohol and the Mind

A person who must have alcohol is an *alcoholic*. Alcoholism is a disease. Alcoholics lose control of their lives. They destroy their families and themselves.

Alcohol is a drug. It affects the central nervous system. Alcohol changes the mood. Just a few drinks can cause changes in behavior.

One or two drinks may cause a person to become loud and silly. More drinks cause drunkenness and loss of control. Drinking may bring about anger, depression, and violent behavior.

Continued heavy drinking affects the central nervous system. Even small amounts of alcohol cause changes in vision.

Alcohol is a legal drug that is readily available—but not for people who are under age.

Driving after drinking is very dangerous. It becomes difficult to track moving objects and to distinguish colors.

The brain is a memory bank. It stores information. Alcohol causes the brain to lose its storing power. Alcoholics may forget large blocks of time. In many alcoholics memory loss becomes permanent. Heavy drinking can damage brain cells. Seizures may occur. Judgment becomes poor. The longer a person drinks, the greater the damage.

Alcohol and Pregnancy

Children of alcoholic mothers may be born with defects. Among defects that have been identified are small head, mental retardation, deformed face and body, and slow growth. This group of defects is called *fetal alcohol syndrome*. Pregnant women must not drink alcohol. Nursing mothers should not drink; alcohol is passed to the baby through breast milk.

Alcohol and Other Drugs

Mixing alcohol with other drugs is dangerous; it is the leading cause of deaths from drugs. Alcohol-drug combinations cause poisoning and overdose.

Alcohol and marijuana taken together are dangerous. The combination interferes with vision. Emergencies need quick response. The alcohol-marijuana combination slows response time. Abusers often become sleepy while driving. They are dangerous on the road.

Alcohol Withdrawal

Heavy drinkers often become alcoholics. Alcoholics cannot stop drinking easily. Sudden withdrawal causes a condition called *delirium tremens*. DTs causes hallucinations. The person talks wildly. Muscles in the arms and legs tighten. High fever occurs. DTs is a medical emergency.

Often the first addiction children succumb to is nicotine—and it is one of the hardest to break.

CHAPTER 13

How Does Tobacco Threaten Health?

*A*lcohol and tobacco are drugs. They are sold legally to adults. Sale to minors is illegal. Yet adolescents drink and smoke. Both alcohol and tobacco are addictive.

Tobacco is grown in the United States. Cigarettes are made from tobacco leaves. So are pipe tobacco, cigars, and chewing tobacco. The use of any tobacco product damages health. Cigarettes present the greatest danger.

Nicotine

Cigarettes contain nicotine, which is a poison. Nicotine is carried by the blood to all the body organs.

Nicotine affects the nerves in the hands. You have probably noticed the shaking

56 hands of heavy smokers. Nicotine affects the eyes, interfering with night vision.

Nicotine causes constipation by hindering the function of the bowel muscles. It acts on the stomach wall, causing ulcers. It increases the heartbeat and the blood pressure. Even the bladder is affected.

Tars

Cigarette smoke contains solid materials in very small pieces called specks. Moisture in the bronchial tubes and lungs changes the specks into sticky substances called tars. Tars clog the air sacs so that oxygen cannot get through.

Respiratory System

Your *respiratory* system lets you breathe. Air taken in through the nose or mouth travels into the lungs.

The lining of the lungs is made of special cells. These cells are designed to stop specks of dust from entering the respiratory system. When the cells are damaged by cigarette smoke they cannot work..

These changed cells also may turn into cancer cells. Lung cancer is the leading cause of death among cigarette smokers.

Nicotine is addictive. Breaking the smoking habit is hard. But it can be broken. If you don't smoke, don't start.

CHAPTER 14

Staying away from Drugs

*D*rugs are all around you. The size of your city or town does not matter. Drugs are there and ready for you. You have to make up your mind. Do you want a chemical substance controlling your life? Or do you want a life that you control.

Feeling Good

People take drugs to feel good. Many young people feel bad about themselves. They cannot handle the stresses of everyday living. Sometimes family trouble causes the stress. Perhaps a parent drinks too much, or there is not enough money. Many young people feel stress in school. Learning is hard and demanding. Often the need for friends causes stress.

57

58   Feeling good about one's self is not always easy. Deep down you may hurt inside. Drugs will not cure that hurt. When the high is gone, the hurt is still there. Growing up is very hard. You have to overcome stress. Strive to feel good. Drugs are not the answer.

Peer Pressure

Peer pressure is the force that friends may put upon you to do something. One of those pressures may be to smoke pot or take pills. If you care a lot about being part of the group, you might follow. If you care more about yourself, you can stand strong and refuse drugs. You must *think*. What will happen to your life if you decide on drugs?

Drinking, smoking, and use of drugs may be started in the home. If parents smoke, teenagers are likely to take up the habit. If parents drink, so may the children. Recent studies show that teenagers take drugs if their parents do. Many drug dealers come from drug-abusing homes.

Coping Skills

Coping is a very special word. It has to do with overcoming problems. How might you cope with things that trouble you?

You want to feel better inside. You are
lonely and depressed. You do not feel as
bright and beautiful as you would like. Do
something useful. Volunteer in your hos-
pital to help the sick children or the eld-
erly. You feel good when you help others.
Help in your place of worship. Your ser-
vices are always needed.

Join a fitness program. Try dancing or
weight lifting or martial arts. With your
doctor's approval, you might begin to jog.
Get some others together and form a walking club.

Develop some skill with your hands.
Take typing, cooking, or woodworking, or
sewing. Find out if you have talent in art,
or photography, or poster-making.

Do you like to sing? Choruses are always looking for new members. Find a
group where you can learn to play a musi-
cal instrument. Ask your school guidance
counselor to put you in touch with activities.

Glossary
Explaining New Words

addict Person who must use drugs several times a day.

amphetamines Drugs that stimulate the central nervous system.

barbiturates Drugs that depress the central nervous system.

drugs Substances not used as medicines that change the mood.

drug abuse Intentional taking of a substance to get high.

drug-dependence Use of drugs to solve problems.

hooked Slang term for being addicted.

illegal drugs Drugs not permitted by law for sale or use.

legal drugs Drugs allowed to be sold by law.

natural drugs Drugs obtained from plants.

pharmacologist Scientist who develops formulas for medicine.

prescription drugs Drugs prescribed as medication by a doctor.

psychoactive drugs Drugs that change a person's behavior.

synthetic drugs Drugs made from chemicals; not natural.

Help List

1-800-COCAINE
Cocaine Helpline
Monday through Friday
9:00 a.m.–3:00 a.m.
Saturday and Sunday
12:00 noon–3:00 a.m.

1-800-554-KIDS
National Federation of
    Parents for Drug-Free
    Youth
Monday through Friday
9:00 a.m.–5:00 p.m.

1-800-662-HELP
National Institute on
    Drug Abuse
Information and
    Referral Line
Monday through Friday
8:30 a.m.–4:30 p.m.

1-800-622-2255
National Council on
    Alcoholism
7 days a week, 24 hours
    a day

You may wish to write to:

National Clearinghouse
    for Alcohol and Drug
    Information
P.O. Box 2345
Rockville, MD 20852
(301) 468-2600

AlAnon/Alateen
    Headquarters
P.O. Box 862, Midtown
    Station
New York, NY 10018
(212) 302-72409

Alcoholics Anonymous
Box 459, Grand Central
    Station
New York, NY 10163

American Council for
    Drug Education
204 Monroe Street
Rockville, MD 20850
(302) 294-0600

Cocanon Family
    Groups
P.O. Box 64742-66
Los Angeles, CA 90064
(213) 859-2206

National Prevention
    Network
444 North Capitol
    Street NW
Washington, DC 20001

For Further Reading

Ball, Jacqueline. *Everything You Need to Know About Drug Abuse.* New York: Rosen Publishing Group, 1990.

Edwards, Gabrielle. *Coping with Drug Abuse.* New York: Rosen Publishing Group, 1990.

Godfrey, Martin. *Heroin.* New York: Franklin Watts, 1987.

Jackson, Michael and Brude. *Doing Drugs.* New York: St. Martin's Press, 1983.

Kaplan, Leslie. *Coping with Peer Pressure.* New York: Rosen Publishing Group, 1990.

Lee, Essie E. *Breaking the Connection.* New York: Julian Messner, 1988.

McFarland, Rhoda. *Coping with Substance Abuse.* New York: Rosen Publishing Group, 1990.

Morgan, H. Wayne. *Drugs in America.* New York: Syracuse University Press, 1981.

Smith, Sandra Lee. *Coping With Decision-Making.* New York: Rosen Publishing Group, 1989.

———. *Value of Sel-Control.* New York: Rosen Publishing Group, 1990.

Sunshine, Linda; Wright, John. *The Best Treatment Centers for Alcoholism and Drug Abuse.* New York: Avon Books, 1988.

Index

63

64

About the Author

Mrs. Gabrielle I. Edwards was Assistant Principal Supervision of the Science Department at Franklin D. Roosevelt High School in Brooklyn. She supervised science instruction for 3,200 young people.

The educator/author devotes much of her time and energy to the improvement of educational experiences and opportunities for young people.

Mrs. Edwards is the author of several books for students in junior and senior high school, including *Coping with Drug Abuse, Biology the Easy Way,* and *Living Things* (co-authored).

Photo Credits

Cover photo: Chris Volpe
Photo on page 2: Gamma Liaison/Frank Fisher; page 7: Wide World; pages 8, 11, 12, 16, 21, 24, 26, 29, 36, 42, 52: Chris Volpe; page 31: Chuck Peterson/Blackbirch Graphics; page 32: Gamma Liaison/John Chiasson; page 54: Stuart Rabinowitz.

Design and Production: Blackbirch Graphics, Inc.

DATE DUE			

14774 REFERENCE

362.29 Edwards, Gabrielle I
Ed

    Drugs on your
    streets

Library Media Center
Madison Central School
Madison, N.Y., 13402

 GUMDROP BOOKS - Bethany, Missouri